Salamanders

Salamanders

by Cherie Winner

A Carolrhoda Nature Watch Book

 Carolrhoda Books, Inc./Minneapolis

For Bob

Special thanks to Dr. J. Eric Juterbock of
The Ohio State University-Lima for clarifying
several important details. Thanks also to
James E. Gerholdt, The Remarkable Reptiles.

This book is available in two editions:
Library binding by Carolrhoda Books, Inc.
Soft cover by First Avenue Editions
241 First Avenue North
Minneapolis, MN 55401

LIBRARY OF CONGRESS CATALOGING-IN-PUBLICATION DATA

Winner, Cherie.
 Salamanders / by Cherie Winner.
  p.   cm.
 "A Carolrhoda nature watch book."
 Includes index.
 Summary: Describes the physical characteristics,
habitat, and life cycle of salamanders.
 ISBN 0-87614-757-0 (lib. bdg.)
 ISBN 0-87614-571-3 (pbk.)
 1. Salamanders—Juvenile literature. [1. Salamanders.]
I. Title.
QL668.C2W55   1993
597.6′5—dc20   92-10430
                                    CIP
                                    AC

Manufactured in the United States of America

1 2 3 4 5 6 98 97 96 95 94 93

Salamanders shed their skin as they grow. Usually the old skin peels off a bit at a time, but sometimes it comes off in one piece, as shown here.

4

Red-backed salamander
(Plethodon cinereus)

For hundreds of years, many people believed that salamanders were magical. In England in the Middle Ages (A.D. 450 to 1450), people thought that fire created salamanders. When they set fire to damp logs, dozens of the slimy creatures scurried out. The word *salamander,* in fact, comes from a Greek word meaning "fire animal." People didn't know that the salamanders lived in the logs and were driven out by the heat.

We now know a lot more about where these shy, quiet creatures come from, how they live, and the important role they play in nature by eating insects and worms. The more than 350 **species**, or types, of salamander are remarkably different. Yet they also share many similarities.

Northern red salamander (Pseudotriton ruber ruber)

Salamanders resemble lizards, with their short legs, long bodies, and long tails. But they are very different from lizards and other **reptiles.** All species of salamander belong to a class of animals called **amphibians.** *Amphi* is an ancient Greek word that means "both." *Amphibian* refers to the fact that these animals spend part of their lives in water and part on land. The young of many species of salamander live like fish; they are great swimmers and can breathe underwater with gills. As adults, many species live on land. They return to the water only to **breed,** or produce offspring. In some species of salamander, however, the adults never leave the water, and in others, they never leave the land.

Those species that live in water all or most of their lives are known as **aquatic** salamanders. Many breathe through gills. They also have lungs and can breathe by sticking their snouts up out of the water. Their lungs have another function, too: they help salamanders stay at a certain depth in the water. The more air salamanders hold in their lungs, the more they float; with less air in their lungs, they tend to sink.

Aquatic salamanders also breathe through their skin. Because their skin is very thin, oxygen in the water is able to pass through the skin into tiny blood vessels called **capillaries.** From there, red blood cells carry the oxygen to the rest of the body. Common aquatic salamanders you may have heard of are the mudpuppy and the waterdog.

Gills, located just behind the head, help this mudpuppy (Necturis maculosus) *breathe underwater.*

This red-backed salamander is a member of the family Plethodontidae.

Those species that live most or all of their lives on land are known as **terrestrial** salamanders. Some even climb and live in trees. Although many of them have lungs, they do much of their breathing through their moist, thin skin. Their skin, like that of most aquatic salamanders, contains many capillaries close to the surface. Oxygen from the air first passes through the water clinging to the skin and then through the skin itself into the capillaries. If the skin dries out, the salamander won't get enough oxygen and will die.

Some terrestrial salamanders do not have lungs. They breathe only through their skin and the moist tissue on the inside of their mouths. These salamanders belong to the family Plethodontidae (pleth-oh-DON-ti-day).

The orange patches on the sides of this Chinese newt (Tylototriton verrucosus)
*are poisonous skin glands. When attacked, the newt lifts its ribs beneath the patches
to make it more likely that the predator will touch the poison.*

Another family of salamander is the Salamandridae, commonly known as **newts.** Most of the newts in the western United States are terrestrial, returning to streams and ponds only during breeding season. Their babies start out in the water but eventually move to land like their parents. These include the California, red-bellied, and rough-skinned newts. Most newts in the eastern United States are aquatic, although they may live on land at one stage in their lives. The Eastern spotted newt (also called the Eastern newt or red-spotted newt), for example, lays its eggs in ponds. A few months after hatching, the young newts crawl out onto land. At this stage, they are called **efts.** The efts live on land, eating and growing, for one to three years. Then, when they become adults, they return to the water.

Eastern spotted newt (Notophthalmus viridescens)

Both aquatic and terrestrial species of salamander come in many sizes. The aquatic giant salamanders of Asia grow to over 5 feet (1.5 m) long and weigh nearly 90 pounds (41 kg). Some other aquatic species grow up to 3 feet (.9 m) long. Terrestrial salamanders are generally smaller; the world's largest is the tiger salamander, which can be 13½ inches (34 cm) long. Some of the terrestrial Thorius (THOR-ee-us) salamanders that live in Mexico are just a bit longer than an inch (2.7 cm).

Whether big or small, and whether they spend all or just part of their lives in the water, salamanders are graceful, fast swimmers. They use their tails like paddles to propel themselves through the water. They also tuck their legs in close to their bodies to move through the water more smoothly. Even terrestrial salamanders can swim if they have to.

On land, though, all salamanders look awkward. Their short, stubby legs stick out to the side and are barely long enough to keep their bellies off the ground. When salamanders walk, they flex their bodies back and forth and wriggle forward.

Salamanders are found in North America, Central America, South America, Europe, Asia, and northern Africa. In general, species living on one continent are not found on others. Some species have a very large **range**—they are found over a large area, such as the entire eastern United States. Other species have a very small range. For example, the terrestrial Kern Canyon slender salamanders live only on the south side of the Kern River Canyon in southern California.

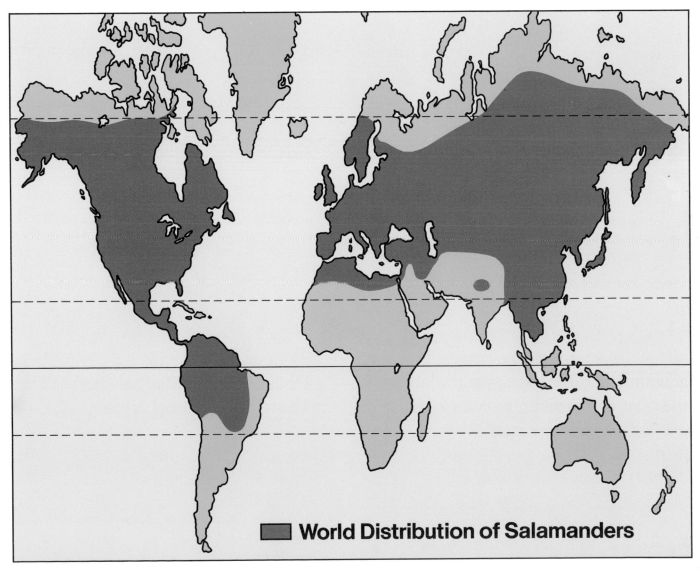

World Distribution of Salamanders

Since all salamanders are **ectotherms** (EK-toh-therms), their body temperature depends on the temperature of their environment. Some people call ectotherms cold-blooded animals, but their blood isn't really cold. Ectotherms cannot produce heat for themselves. They also cannot cool themselves. Both on land and in water, salamanders depend on sun, shade, and shelter to maintain their proper body temperature.

In winter, terrestrial salamanders burrow into the ground or into cracks in rotting logs. Aquatic salamanders survive winter by staying near the bottom of their pond or stream, away from the ice that may form on the surface. Sometimes they burrow into the mud bottom. In spring, they swim up close to the surface of the water to soak up warmth from the sun.

A slimy salamander (Plethodon glutinosus) *suns itself in early spring. In warmer months, slimy salamanders are found on the shady forest floor.*

Wet leaves and bark protect this spotted salamander (Ambystoma maculatum) *from cool weather.*

In summer, salamanders must find shelter from the sun. They also must stay in a place that is damp so their skin won't dry out. For aquatic salamanders, staying moist is easy; they live in the water. When the water near the surface of their pond gets too warm, they swim deeper, to where the water is cool.

During the warm months, terrestrial salamanders live under the leaves on the forest floor, in soggy rotting logs, or in burrows. These burrows can be up to 3 feet (.9 m) deep. Some may be even deeper. At such depths, even in dry climates, the soil is moist enough to allow the salamanders to breathe.

When it comes to food, salamanders are **carnivores.** They eat other animals. Terrestrial salamanders eat worms, insects, snails, and, occasionally, small mice. Aquatic salamanders eat insects, small fish, tadpoles, and even other salamanders.

Most aquatic salamanders hover in the water until a tasty-looking snack comes by. Then they snap open their wide mouths so quickly that the water and prey rush into their mouths. Then they slam their mouths shut and swallow the prey.

On land, terrestrial salamanders sometimes wait for prey to wander by. More often, they actively hunt for their food.

Salamanders have several rows of sharp teeth on the roof of their mouth. These teeth are made of materials called dentine and enamel, the same materials human teeth are made of, but they don't crush and chew food like human teeth do. They help salamanders keep animals from escaping once they're caught. Salamanders gulp their food and digest it in their stomachs.

A spotted salamander makes a tasty meal of a worm.

If a salamander can't find enough to eat, it might starve or be forced to travel great distances to find food. Along the way, it may run into **predators,** such as herons, snakes, fish, and foxes. To avoid being eaten by predators, most species of salamander try to avoid being noticed. Whether in water or on land, they stay under leaves, logs, or rocks much of the time. Since salamanders are also very quiet, a predator can walk or swim right past them without suspecting they're there.

No one is sure how long individual salamanders can live in the wild. Some kept in zoos have lived more than 50 years. There, salamanders are protected from extreme weather, food shortages, and predators.

A red-backed salamander falls prey to an Eastern garter snake (Thamnophis sirtalis sirtalis).

An adult Eastern spotted newt (above) has a dark green back and a yellow belly.
As a juvenile (right), called a red eft, the Eastern newt is bright red-orange.

Salamanders of all kinds have unique abilities that help them survive in their environment. These special abilities are called **adaptations.** They help an animal adapt to, or fit in with, its surroundings. Some adaptations involve behavior, such as staying hidden and being quiet. Others involve the structure of parts of the body. The colors of salamanders are a good example of adaptation. They often help salamanders blend with their surroundings, so they are hard to see.

Most aquatic salamanders are drab brown or olive green. Some are dark on their backs and light on their bellies. This coloring is known as **counter-shading.** When seen from above, these salamanders blend in with the dark bottom of the pond. When seen from below (for example, by a hungry fish), they blend in with the bright sky above them.

Eastern spotted newts are different colors at different times of their lives. Just after hatching, they are greenish brown. When they move onto land as efts, they are bright red-orange, with red spots on their backs. When they return to the water as adults, they become one of the few aquatic salamanders that is brightly colored. As adults, they also have countershading—their bellies are yellow and their backs are dark, shiny green. Many black spots and two rows of red or orange spots also decorate their backs. Just as a person's fingerprints are unique, the pattern of spots is unique to each individual newt.

Some terrestrial salamanders are drab, but others are bright green, red, blue, or gold. They may have spots or stripes, or they may be a solid color.

California newt
(Taricha torosa)

You might think that the bright colors of some salamander species would attract predators. In fact, most salamander species with flashy colors try hard to show those colors when a predator approaches. They raise their chins and tails so the vivid colors on their undersides show. For these salamanders, the colors advertise a special weapon that is another kind of adaptation—poisonous skin. The skin of just one California newt, for example, contains enough poison in its **skin glands** to kill several foxes. Glands are groups of special cells that secrete substances through pores in the skin.

Since a predator must eat the California newt to be poisoned, this weapon doesn't actually protect the newt that is attacked. But it protects other California newts—if the predator dies, it won't hunt anymore. Even if the predator doesn't die, it will get so sick that it will avoid eating brightly colored salamanders in the future!

The skin glands of the California slender salamander have adapted in a slightly different way. California slenders are 3 to 5 inches (8 to 14 cm) long and very thin, so they look almost like worms with legs. Rather than making poison as the California newt does, the California slender's glands make a fluid that is so sticky it can glue a snake's mouth shut or the coils of its body together. Once its enemy is stuck, the little salamander can slither away. Sometimes, though, the snake swallows the salamander before it has a chance to secrete the fluid.

The California slender salamander (Batrachoseps attenuatus) *spends most of its life in burrows dug by earthworms.*

Some salamanders have a remarkable way of defending themselves when attacked—they make their own tail fall off. This adaptation is called **autotomy** (aw-TAH-toh-my). It's a good strategy because the tail continues to wiggle for several minutes after it falls off. Since most predators prefer moving **prey,** the squirming tail keeps their attention. This allows the salamander to slip away from harm.

Autotomy is not a permanent loss for the salamander, because its tail will **regenerate,** or grow back. Many salamanders, both aquatic and terrestrial, can regenerate parts of their body that have been lost or badly injured. Many can regenerate their legs and tail and make a perfect copy of the original part. Depending on its age, size, and species, a salamander can grow back an entire limb in 2 to 10 weeks. Smaller, younger salamanders regenerate body parts more quickly than larger, older ones.

The ensatina (Ensatina eschscholtzi) below has just autotomized its tail. The slimy salamander on the right is in the process of regenerating its autotomized tail. You can see where the tail came off because the new tail is a lighter color. Eventually, it will match the rest of the salamander's body.

A regenerating limb first looks like a cone. The cone grows longer and longer, and then flattens at the end where the foot will be. Finally, the smooth border at the tip of this flattened cone develops dents, which will become the spaces between the toes. Salamanders can swim, walk, or do anything else with the regenerated limb that they were able to do with the original limb.

Some salamanders can also grow back parts of the jaw, liver, spinal cord, and even the lens of the eye. Biologists all over the world are studying various species of salamander to learn how they are able to regenerate missing body parts. If scientists can discover how salamanders are able to do this, they may be able to help people who suffer from crippling injuries.

Salamanders' senses have also adapted to help them survive. Salamanders don't have visible "ear holes" or flaps of tissue for ears. But the parts of their ears inside their heads work very much like humans' ears do. Just as you can hear something even if you plug your ears, salamanders can hear even though they have no ear holes.

Aquatic salamanders have another way of sensing when another creature is nearby. They can "hear" through a structure called the **lateral line organ.** This organ runs in a line down each side of a salamander's body and in several lines on its head. The organ senses vibrations in the water, such as those a heron makes when stalking a salamander. The lateral line organ enables the salamander to figure out how big the source of vibrations is and how far away it is.

Salamanders living on land have only internal ears. They do not have lateral line organs. Species of terrestrial salamander that start life in water and later move to land have a lateral line organ while their home is in water. When they move to a home on land, they lose the use of this organ. But they can sense vibrations coming through the ground through their toes.

The Pacific giant salamander (Dicamptodon ensatus) may grow to 12 inches long (30 cm), not including its tail. It eats mice, other salamanders, and garter snakes.

The cave salamander (Eurycea lucifuga) lives near the mouths of caves where there is some light, so it is able to see to navigate and find food.

Salamanders are usually very quiet. They don't call, croak, or grunt, as frogs do. However, the Pacific giant salamander, an aquatic salamander, makes a sound like a bark. Even though most salamanders don't make sounds often, they do communicate with one another. They rely on two senses to get their messages across: sight and smell.

On land, neither aquatic nor terrestrial salamanders see as well as people do. Salamanders recognize specific objects near them. With more distant objects, they just see movement or large areas of dark and light. They have little need for distance vision since they live in small areas on the forest floor close to their prey. Aquatic salamanders can see much better under water than on land.

The European blind salamander relies primarily on its sense of smell to find its way around and to hunt for food. These unusual aquatic salamanders live in permanent darkness in underground streams in the Alps of Italy and in south-eastern Europe (the area formerly called Yugoslavia). They grow to be up to 1 foot (30 cm) long and are whitish or very pale gray, pink, or yellow. They are blind because their eyes never fully develop. Even if they're brought into the light, their eyes don't function.

The nose of a salamander doesn't look like much from the outside—just two small nostrils on its blunt snout—but it works well. Most species of salamander have glands in their skin that secrete fluids that other salamanders can smell and recognize. For example, when a California newt meets another salamander, it can tell by how the newcomer smells and acts whether the other salamander is also a California newt or some other species. It can also tell whether the stranger is a male or female.

Notice the nostril on this salamander's blunt snout.

Northern red salamanders, like most salamanders, are solitary animals that come together only during breeding season. They live their entire lives in or near the small streams where they themselves were hatched.

Recognizing potential mates is important for salamanders to successfully reproduce. Some species, such as the California newt, do this primarily through the sense of smell. In other species, the male develops unusual color patterns during the breeding season. The male European crested newt, a terrestrial salamander that returns to the water to breed, has a crest along his back year-round. As breeding season approaches, his crest gets bigger and his dark skin fades in places. Eventually, he turns gray with big black patches all over, smaller white spots on his sides, and a blue-white stripe on his tail. These colors tell females that the male is ready to mate.

Aquatic salamanders, and terrestrial salamanders that breed on land, find their mates close to home. While they tend to live alone and avoid other salamanders most of the time, during breeding season, the males and females seek each other out.

Terrestrial salamanders that breed in water also keep to themselves during most of the year. But to mate, once a year they go on an overland **migration,** or trip, back to their breeding pond. Hundreds or even thousands of salamanders make the trip, but only a few may be seen at one time. Once in the pond, the males and females court, mate, and produce offspring. In areas where several species share a breeding pond, different species migrate together.

This pond, called a vernal pool, forms each spring when rain water fills a low area. During this time, it serves as a breeding ground for migrating salamanders.

Migrating salamanders move great distances and return to the exact pond or stretch of stream where they were hatched. Even if you move terrestrial salamanders far from their starting point, they find their way back to their birth pond. Some California newts that scientists tested traveled more than 9 miles (14.5 km) over two large hills to reach their birth stream. Aquatic salamanders usually live near the place where they were hatched, so they don't migrate as terrestrial salamanders do.

Salamanders use their sense of smell to find their birth homes. Small animals, plants, and soils all have distinctive odors, which salamanders can follow. Young salamanders rapidly learn to recognize the pattern of odors at the place where they were hatched. This learning process is called **imprinting.** Salamanders seek out this pattern of odors during all of their later migrations.

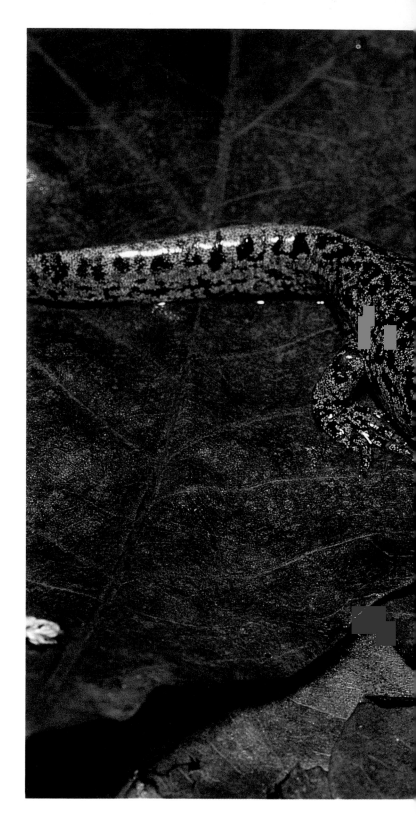

In the spring, mole salamanders (Ambystoma talpoideum) *come out of their homes underground to migrate to their breeding ponds.*

Migrating salamanders that are far away from their homes encounter many dangers. Exposure to predators is one. Some of their predators are active only during the day, however. Since the salamanders tend to move at night, most get back to their birth ponds safely.

Harsh weather is also dangerous for migrating salamanders. Most species migrate with the first warm rains of spring. Usually, no more frost occurs after the rains start. Sometimes, though, a late freeze can kill the migrating salamanders.

The migration can be so exhausting that some species of salamander make the trip to breed only every other year. This is especially true of the females. After mating, terrestrial salamanders leave the breeding pond. As far as scientists know, they return to the same area they lived in before coming to the pond.

These Western red-backed salamanders (Plethodon vehiculum) *are performing a mating dance. They breed on land and do not migrate.*

In most species of salamander, both aquatic and terrestrial, mating involves a dance, the release of **sperm,** and then **fertilization** (the binding of sperm and **egg**) inside the body of the female. Each species has its own special dance, but generally, when a male finds a potential mate, he moves in front of her and waves his tail. This pushes his own scent toward her. It also signals that he wants to mate. If the female salamander wants to mate, she joins him in a courtship dance. They swim or walk beside and around each other. They often hit each other with their heads as well.

These three spermatophores were deposited on leaves in shallow water. The sperm are located at the top of each sticky lump.

In most species, when the female salamander is ready to mate, the male deposits a bundle of sperm, called a **spermatophore** (sper-MAT-oh-for), on a rock or stick and guides the female to the bundle. As she rubs over the sperm, they enter her body through an opening beneath her tail. Inside her body, the sperm fertilize her eggs. The male may then court other females.

In some species, the male embraces the female by hugging her body with either his front or hind legs. The male Eastern spotted newt has very rough, black patches of skin called **nuptial pads** on the insides of his hind legs that help him hug the female. He also has rough patches on his hind toes, called **claspers.** Nuptial pads and claspers develop as the male is getting ready to breed. After the breeding season, they fade and disappear.

In a few aquatic species, the female releases her eggs first. Then the male releases his sperm right on top of the eggs. Fertilization occurs in the water.

The female that just mated finds a good place to lay her fertilized eggs, which are now **embryos,** or developing young. To anchor them in a particular spot, she often attaches them to a stick or rock.

Just as adult salamanders must keep moist to survive, so must their fertilized eggs. For this reason, females lay their eggs either in water (aquatic salaman- ders and terrestrial species that return to water to breed) or in moist areas on land (terrestrial salamanders that do not return to water to breed). A few species don't lay eggs at all. The female black salamander, a terrestrial species, carries her fertilized eggs inside her until they finish developing. Then she gives birth to live young.

A spotted salamander attached these embryos to a stick underwater. Clear egg jelly surrounds them.

Some female salamanders that breed in ponds lay just a few eggs, one or two at a time. Others can lay up to several hundred eggs in one breeding season. Around and among the eggs is a clear **egg jelly.** This jelly protects the embryos and helps the whole group of eggs stick together. Egg jelly swells quickly once it's in the water. A mass of eggs as big as a grapefruit may come from a single salamander only as big as your index finger. Eggs laid on land are usually surrounded by a thin layer of egg jelly.

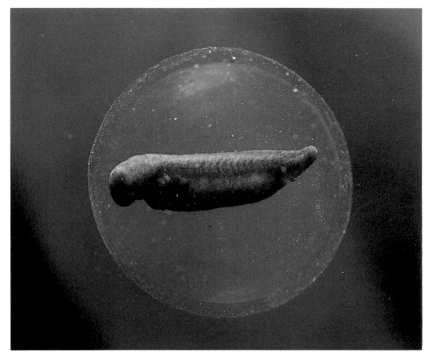

Each embryo develops within its own egg case (above). The round embryo gradually becomes longer and thinner. When it hatches as a larva, approximately three weeks later (below), its tail, gills, and eyes are well developed.

Each salamander egg is a ball about ¹⁄₁₀ of an inch (2 to 3 mm) across. It does not have a hard outer shell. The embryo is nourished during its growth by the yolk, which contains proteins, carbohydrates, and other nutrients. This yolk is not a yellow ball like the yolk in chicken eggs. Rather, it is pale gray and is stored in the cells that will make up the digestive system of the embryo.

Since salamander eggs don't have an outer shell, they are easy to watch develop. Biologists study them to learn how the yolk and other materials in the egg provide for the developing baby. They also study how organs, such as the spinal cord, heart, and kidneys, form.

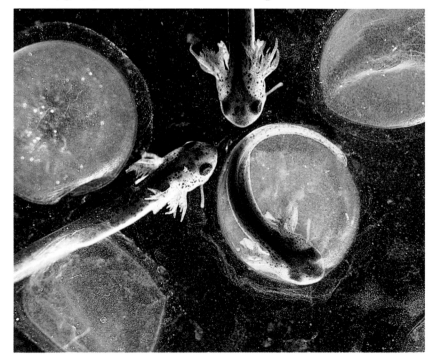

The four-toed salamander (Hemidactylium scutatum) *guards her embryos until they hatch, which takes from 1 to 2 months.*

Often, many different kinds of salamanders breed in the same small pond. In spring, the whole pond may be filled with embryos. These embryos take from three weeks to several months to hatch. This is an especially dangerous time for the salamanders. Salamander embryos are sensitive to environmental stress, such as pollution. And since the embryos can't fight, run, or hide, they make an easy meal for hungry predators. In most species of aquatic salamander, the female guards her embryos until they hatch. Terrestrial species that breed in water usually don't tend their embryos.

One of the few cases in which male salamanders care for the developing embryos is the aquatic Japanese giant salamander. The female lays her eggs in two long rows, like beads on a string, beneath rocks in the water or in holes dug by the male. The male then stays near the eggs and fans the water around them with his tail. Moving the water around adds more oxygen to the water for the embryos.

For those species of terrestrial salamander that breed on land, the biggest problem is keeping themselves and their embryos wet. Female Dusky salamanders bury themselves with their eggs under logs or rocks. The mother wraps herself around her clutch of 10 to 30 eggs until they hatch. This takes up to three months. During that time, the mother doesn't eat or drink. She absorbs moisture from the damp earth, and her presence in the burrow keeps the embryos from drying out. She also fights off intruders, and she eats any of her embryos that die. If she didn't do that, the dead embryos could get moldy and infect the rest of her babies. When the eggs hatch, the youngsters squirm to the nearest stream or pond, usually 5 to 10 feet (1.5 to 3 m) away. Then they are on their own. Their mother stays on land.

A Northern dusky salamander (Desmognathus fuscus fuscus) *guards her eggs.*

A spotted salamander larva

Most terrestrial salamanders that breed on land have babies that look just like smaller versions of adults. They are the same color as the adults, and they do not have gills.

Terrestrial salamander babies that are born in water don't look much like their parents. These babies, called **larvae** (LAR-vee), have large featherlike gills at the back of their heads, small legs, and duller coloring than their parents. Larvae spend the first few months of their lives in the water, where they eat small animals, such as plankton (microscopic animals). Some larvae also eat algae. As they eat, the larvae grow up to several inches long. They stay in the water and breathe mostly through their skin and gills.

In late summer, larvae go through a drastic change called **metamorphosis.** This enables them to leave the water and live on land. Their gills shrink and finally disappear. Their bodies and legs become much stronger so they can support themselves on land. Their skin changes, too. It gets thicker and eventually turns the colors characteristic of the species. For all the changes it involves, metamorphosis doesn't take very long—from a few days to a few weeks.

The metamorphosed salamander is now a juvenile and usually stays on land. It still has some growing to do before becoming a mature adult and able to breed. That can take from one to eight years, depending on the species.

Some aquatic salamanders also metamorphose. For example, the Eastern spotted newts' larvae metamorphose to become efts that leave the water and live on land for one to three years before returning to the pond as adults.

Some Eastern tiger salamander larvae (Ambystoma tigrinum tigrinum), *like the one below, will metamorphose to become terrestrial adults like the one on the right. Others never metamorphose.*

Many other aquatic salamanders never leave the water and never metamorphose. These salamanders are called **neotenic** (nee-oh-TEN-ick). They become adults and are able to breed even though they still look much like larvae. Most of them keep their gills throughout life. Mudpuppies, hellbenders, and axolotls are common neotenic salamanders.

Tiger salamanders aren't all neotenic or metamorphosed. Those in one pond may metamorphose (and become terrestrial), while all those from a pond just ¼ mile (.4 km) away may remain neotenic. No one knows why. Neotenic tiger salamanders are sometimes called waterdogs.

The mudpuppy is a neotenic salamander. Its feathery gills look dark-red because they contain thousands of capillaries to help it breathe.

Some people also call neotenic tiger salamanders axolotls. But the name *axolotl* really belongs to a Mexican salamander. It is closely related to the tiger salamander. Axolotls come from a mountain lake in central Mexico and are always neotenic. They come in a wide range of colors, from white to yellow to dark green.

Scientists raise axolotls in laboratories to study embryonic development and limb regeneration. One of the biggest and most famous of these breeding colonies is at Indiana University in Bloomington. Sometimes scientists also use axolotl and tiger salamander embryos to test water from different ponds or streams. If the water harms the embryos, it might also be dangerous for other wild animals or for humans.

As pollution and growing human populations destroy salamanders' natural habitats (areas where salamanders normally live), some species are nearly dying out. They are considered **threatened** or **endangered** in some parts of the world.

Ensuring breeding is crucial for many species, particularly those that are already threatened or endangered and nearing **extinction**. One such salamander is the Eastern tiger salamander. You can still find them in Ohio and Maryland, but not in Pennsylvania—they haven't been seen there since the 1930s. For many kinds of salamander, we do not yet know how much space is needed or how many individuals must live in one area for them to breed successfully.

We damage salamanders' habitats when we build roads near salamanders' ponds and streams. Migrating salamanders then have no choice but to cross the pavement. Sometimes you can see as many as several hundred salamanders on a road at one time! One car driving down the road at the peak of migration could kill most of the salamanders returning to one pond. This is also dangerous for drivers, since squashed salamanders are slippery enough to make a car skid out of control.

Migrating salamanders will be unable to breed in this polluted stream.

Some towns, such as Brecksville, Ohio, near Cleveland, now protect salamanders during migration. If people don't often use the road the salamanders use, or if there are easy detours around the road, the town closes the road to car traffic. Then the salamanders have the road all to themselves.

If the town has to keep the road open, volunteers patrol its edges. When the crossing guards find a migrating salamander, they either stop car traffic until the salamander makes it across the road or pick up the salamander and carry it across.

Building tunnels beneath roads is another way people are helping to protect migrating salamanders. They put up barriers along the roads to prevent the salamanders from stepping onto the pavement and to guide them toward the tunnel openings.

Protecting migrating salamanders is just one example of how people are beginning to help salamanders. As we learn more about salamanders, we can find other ways to help them survive. Much of what we learn can benefit us as well. With the salamanders' help, we can learn to tell if streams have been made unsafe by pollution. And some day, perhaps, we will understand the biggest mystery of all—their ability to regenerate. There is still much that these gentle creatures can teach us.

GLOSSARY

adaptation: a feature of an animal that helps it adapt to, or fit successfully into, its environment

amphibians: the class of vertebrates, or animals with spines, that includes frogs and salamanders. Most of these animals spend part of their lives in water and part on land.

aquatic: living or occuring in water

autotomy: the separation of the tail from the rest of the body to distract a predator

breed: produce offspring

capillaries: small blood vessels. Those located close to the surface of the skin can absorb oxygen from the air.

carnivore: an animal that eats other animals

claspers: rough, dark patches of skin that appear on the hind toes of the males of some species during the breeding season. These patches of skin help the male grip the female during the mating process.

countershading: having different colors on the back than on the belly. This helps an animal blend in with its surroundings.

ectotherms: animals whose body temperature depends on the temperature of their environment. Another word used to describe this condition is *cold-blooded.*

eft: the land-dwelling juvenile of some species of aquatic newt

egg: a female reproductive cell

egg jelly: the clear, jellylike substance that binds many embryos together in a cluster

embryo: an animal in the early stages of development, before birth or hatching

endangered: in danger of becoming extinct

extinction: when no members of a species are left alive

fertilization: the joining of a sperm from the male and an egg from the female to produce a baby

imprinting: programmed or automatic learning that occurs very early in an animal's life, such as when a young salamander learns the pattern of smells in its home pond

larva: a young salamander before metamorphosis

lateral line organ: a vibration-sensing organ located on the head and along the sides of the body of aquatic salamanders and fish

metamorphosis: the drastic physical change that occurs when a salamander larva, which lives in the water, becomes an adult that lives on land. Other animals that metamorphose are tadpoles and caterpillars.

migration: movement from one region to another, usually seasonally, for feeding or breeding

neotenic: adult aquatic salamanders that do not metamorphose

newts: salamanders of the family Salamandridae; some species are aquatic, some are terrestrial

nuptial pads: rough, dark patches of skin that appear on the hind legs of the males of some species during the breeding season. The pads help the male hug the female during the mating process.

predator: an animal that hunts other animals

prey: an animal that is hunted by other animals

range: the geographic area in which a species lives

regenerate: to grow back a body part that has been lost, such as a tail or a leg

reptiles: a class of vertebrates that includes lizards, snakes, turtles, and crocodiles; these animals are covered with scales, do not breathe through their skin, and lay eggs that have a tough outer shell

skin gland: a group of special cells that secrete substances through pores in the skin. In some species, the substance may be poisonous.

species: a group of animals or plants that share similar characteristics and can breed together

sperm: a male reproductive cell

spermatophore: a mass of sperm deposited all at one time

terrestrial: living or occuring on land

threatened: not in immediate danger of extinction but declining in numbers. This may be due to human interference or natural changes in the species' habitat.

INDEX

Diagram on p. 11 by Laura Westlund.
Photographs courtesy of: front cover, pp. 14, 34 (both), 37, © Dwight Kuhn; pp. 2, 7, 20-21, 30, 42 (both), 43, 46, © 1992 Klaus O. Richter; pp. 4, 8, 13, 15, 16, 24, 25, 27, 28-29, © A. B. Sheldon; pp. 5, 6, 17, 33, 36, © John Serrao; pp. 9, 10, 18, 21, 26, 32, 35, 38 (both), 39, 40, back cover, © Breck P. Kent; pp. 12, 31, © Nick Bergkessel 1992; p. 19, © Nicholas A. Cavagnaro; pp. 22-23, © 1991 Jim Yuskavitch; p. 40 (both), Indiana University Axolotl Colony; p. 41, National Association of Conservation Districts.

ABOUT THE AUTHOR

When **Cherie Winner** was introduced to salamanders in graduate school, she was fascinated that they are so invisible to the people who live close to salamanders' habitats. Ms. Winner became so interested in these gentle creatures that she spent more than a decade studying them. She holds a Ph.D. in zoology from Ohio State University and has taught embryology and vertebrate anatomy at the university level. Dr. Winner is now a full-time writer. She lives in Wyoming with her husband, Bob, their cats, Shiloh and Tucker, and their dog, Sheba.